The Joy of
Running

AN INSPIRED COLLECTION
OF QUOTATIONS FOR THOSE
WHO LOVE TO RUN

Arranged by Jackie Corley

THE JOY OF RUNNING

Text Copyright © 2019 Hatherleigh Press

Library of Congress Cataloging-in-Publication Data is available.
ISBN: 978-1-57826-813-9

Printed in the United States
10 9 8 7 6 5 4 3 2 1

CONTENTS

INTRODUCTION

RUNNING IS ONE OF the only sports or exercise regimens that doesn't require expensive equipment or a monthly membership fee. Your body, a willing mind, and a supportive pair of shoes are all that you need to enter into a club that strengthens the muscles and tones the spirit—and this club is a broad one, with diverse members ranging from ultra-marathoners to those training for their first 5K.

The reasons runners decide to take to the pavement are equally broad. For every aspiring Prefontaine or Paula Radcliffe determined to shatter personal records on race day, there are scores of casual runners whose sole focus is relieving stress or maintaining their health.

Whichever type of runner you are, there will come a point when you reach a plateau—or a wall. You may wonder why you can't run faster, why adding another mile feels impossible or if the benefits of running are really worth it. When you find yourself there, consider the words of other runners who have been in your shoes. This collection of encouraging quotations offers advice, humor, and wisdom from athletes and coaches, to presidents and philosophers, that will help you find the motivation you need to get back on your feet and achieve your goals as a runner.

EVERYONE'S AN ATHLETE

YOU DON'T NEED TO FINISH A SIX-minute mile to consider yourself a runner. If you step outside your front door and endeavor to run with any regularity, you're a runner. Our bodies were built to run, and anyone who exercises this ability has earned the right to call themselves an athlete.

Why run? I run because I am an animal. I run because it is part of my genetic wiring. I run because millions of years of evolution have left me programmed to run. And finally, I run because there's no better way to see the sun rise and set.

—AMBY BURFOOT

For every runner who tours the world running marathons, there are thousands who run to hear the leaves and listen to the rain, and look to the day when it is suddenly as easy as a bird in flight.

—GEORGE SHEEHAN

Start where you are. Use what you have. Do what you can.

—Arthur Ashe

If you run, you are a runner. It doesn't matter how fast or how far. It doesn't matter if today is your first day or if you've been running for twenty years. There is no test to pass, no license to earn, no membership card to get. You just run.

—John Bingham

I n running, it doesn't matter whether you come in first, in the middle of the pack, or last. You can say, "I have finished." There is a lot of satisfaction in that.

—FRED LEBOW

I often hear someone say "I'm not a real runner." We are all runners, some just run faster than others. I never met a fake runner.

—BART YASSO

You were born to run. Maybe not that fast, maybe not that far, maybe not as efficiently as others. But to get up and move, to fire up that entire energy-producing, oxygen-delivering, bone-strengthening process we call running.

—FLORENCE GRIFFITH JOYNER

Success is the sum of small efforts, repeated day in and day out.

—ROBERT COLLIER

Believe that you can run farther or faster. Believe that you're young enough, old enough, strong enough, and so on to accomplish everything you want to do. Don't let worn-out beliefs stop you from moving beyond yourself.

—JOHN BINGHAM

I always tell beginning runners: Train your brain first. It's much more important than your heart or legs.

—AMBY BURFOOT

We are designed to run and we increase our chance of daily happiness when we do so.

—JEFF GALLOWAY

What is the purpose of any one workout? Enjoyment? Improvement? Coach said so? Whatever, the hour you run often is the best hour of the day.

—HAL HIGDON

If you don't think you were born to run, you're not only denying history. You're denying who you are.

—CHRISTOPHER MCDOUGALL

Ability is what you're capable of doing. Motivation determines what you do. Attitude determines how well you do it.

—LOU HOLTZ

For me, as for so many runners, there really are no finish lines. Runs end; running doesn't.

—DEAN KARNAZES

The miracle isn't that I finished. The miracle is that I had the courage to start.

—JOHN BINGHAM

Just put one foot in front of the other.

—AUSTIN PECK

Anybody can be a runner. We were meant to move. We were meant to run. It's the easiest sport.

—BILL RODGERS

If you want to become the best runner you can be, start now. Don't spend the rest of your life wondering if you can do it.

—PRISCILLA WELCH

The simplicity of running is the heart and soul of the sport. The ordinary, everyday runners are the mainstream. I can never forget this because I am one of them, regardless of what else I am.

—FRED LEBOW

To know you are one with what you are doing, to know that you are a complete athlete, begins with believing you are a runner.

—GEORGE SHEEHAN

The advice I have for beginners is the same philosophy that I have for runners of all levels of experience and ability—consistency, a sane approach, moderation, and making your running an enjoyable, rather than dreaded, part of your life.

—BILL RODGERS

We may train or peak for a certain race, but running is a lifetime sport.

—ALBERTO SALAZAR

Life is a positive-sum game. Everyone from the gold medalist to the last finisher can rejoice in a personal victory.

—GEORGE SHEEHAN

The athlete defeats fear and conquers himself!

—FRANZ STAMPFL

Some people feel "transformed" from the first day they begin running; others feel that it's just plain hard work. Most of us realize it is both. I know how great running can feel, but I also know it can feel not so great, even downright awful! It can be fun, but it takes work to have that fun.

—GRETE WAITZ

I am a runner because I run. Not because I run fast. Not because I run far. I am a runner because I say I am. And no one can tell me I'm not.

—JOHN BINGHAM

A METAPHOR
FOR LIFE

A RUNNER'S JOURNEY PARALLELS A *life's journey. The struggles and achievements you experience as you progress with running can teach you much about how to live your life to its fullest.*

Running is the greatest metaphor for life, because you get out of it what you put into it.

—Oprah Winfrey

Life is often compared to a marathon, but I think it is more like being a sprinter; long stretches of hard work punctuated by brief moments in which we are given the opportunity to perform at our best.

—Michael Johnson

The five S's of sports training are: stamina, speed, strength, skill, and spirit; but the greatest of these is spirit.

—Ken Doherty

Every time I fail, I assume I will be a stronger person for it. I keep on running figuratively and literally, despite a limp that gets more noticeable with each passing season, because for me there has always been a place to go and a terrible urgency to get there.

—JOAN BENOIT

I've learned that it's what you do with the miles, rather than how many you've run.

—ROD DEHAVEN

Running has taught me, perhaps more than anything else, that there's no reason to fear starting lines...or other new beginnings.

—AMBY BURFOOT

Every morning in Africa, a gazelle wakes up, it knows it must outrun the fastest lion or it will be killed. Every morning in Africa, a lion wakes up. It knows it must run faster than the slowest gazelle, or it will starve. It doesn't matter whether you're the lion or a gazelle – when the sun comes up, you'd better be running.

—CHRISTOPHER McDOUGALL

Running is about finding your inner peace, and so is a life well lived.

—DEAN KARNAZES

Every run is a work of art, a drawing on each day's canvas. Some runs are shouts and some runs are whispers. Some runs are eulogies and others celebrations. When you're angry, a run can be a sharp slap in the face. When happy, a run is your song.

—DAGNY SCOTT BARRIOS

Running is a lot like life. Only 10 percent of it is exciting. 90 percent of it is slog and drudge.

—DAVID BEDFORD

When I do the best I can with what I have, then I have won my race.

—Jay Foonberg

Most runners run not because they want to live longer, but because they want to live life to the fullest.

—Haruki Murakami

Running is not just exercise; it is a lifestyle.

—John Bingham

Some of the world's greatest feats were accomplished by people not smart enough to know they were impossible.

—DOUG LARSON

Racing teaches us to challenge ourselves. It teaches us to push beyond where we thought we could go. It helps us to find out what we are made of. This is what we do. This is what it's all about.

—PATTISUE PLUMER

I run because it's so symbolic of life. You have to drive yourself to overcome the obstacles. You might feel that you can't. But then you find your inner strength, and realize you're capable of so much more than you thought.

—ARTHUR BLANK

Good things come slow, especially in distance running.

—BILL DELLINGER

A lot of people give up when the world seems to be against them, but that's the point when you should push a little harder. I use the analogy of running a race. It seems as though you can't carry on, but if you just get through the pain barrier, you'll see the end and be okay. Often, just around the corner is where the solution will happen.

—JAMES DYSON

It's all about the journey, not the outcome.

— CARL LEWIS

You can't flirt with the track, you must marry it.

—BILL EASTON

I am thankful that there are different seasons in life and training. I have learned to embrace each season, realizing how important it is to allow the body, mind, and spirit to fully cycle through each.

—RYAN HALL

Almost every part of the mile is tactically important: you can never let down, never stop thinking, and you can be beaten at almost any point. I suppose you could say it is like life.

—JOHN LANDY

L ike running, trying to live a good life has to hurt a little bit, or we're not running hard enough, not really trying.

 —JUNE JORDAN

I f you hold back in hurdles, you are going to fall over.

 —SALLY PEARSON

Y ou never know the limit of a human being.
 —ALBERTO JUANTORENA

Remember, the feeling you get from a good run is far better than the feeling you get from sitting around wishing you were running.

—SARAH CONDOR

If you become restless, speed up. If you become winded, slow down. You climb the mountain in an equilibrium between restlessness and exhaustion.

—ROBERT PIRSIG

In many ways, a race is analogous to life itself. Once it is over, it cannot be re-created. All that is left are impressions in the heart and in the mind.

—CHRIS LEAR

Marathoning is a metaphor for life, so there are a lot of parallels you can draw. I tell people to follow your dream, follow your heart, follow your passion, run your own race, and believe in yourself.

—JOAN BENOIT

Experienced runners learn to respect the changing needs of their bodies. That's the wisdom that comes with time, and—for good or bad—with age.

—FRED LEBOW

The body is given out on loan—don't waste it and expect to use it tomorrow.

—CARL SHAPIRO

It's very hard in the beginning to understand that the whole idea is not to beat the other runners. Eventually you learn that the competition is against the little voice inside you that wants you to quit.

—GEORGE SHEEHAN

Bad workouts and races—we all have them and we always will. Accept that the body has an ebb and flow that we don't quite understand.

—GREG MCMILLAN

I f we wait for the moment when everything, absolutely everything, is ready, we shall never begin.

—Ivan Turgenev

I f you train your mind for running, everything else will be easy.

—Amby Burfoot

F or an athlete, the biggest pressure comes from within. You know what you want to do and what you're capable of.

—Paula Radcliffe

The will to win means nothing without the will to prepare.

—JUMA IKANGAA

The point is whether or not I improved over yesterday. In long-distance running the only opponent you have to beat is yourself, the way you used to be.

—HARUKI MURAKAMI

Running is not, as it so often seems, only about what you did in your last race or about how many miles you ran last week. It is, in a much more important way, about community, about appreciating all the miles run by other runners, too.

—RICHARD O'BRIEN

Life (and running) is not all about time but about our experiences along the way.

—JENNIFER RHINES

Workouts are like brushing my teeth; I don't think about them, I just do them. The decision has already been made.

—PattiSue Plumer

I don't run to add days to my life, I run to add life to my days.

—Ronald Rook

Running should be a lifelong activity. Approach it patiently and intelligently, and it will reward you for a long, long time.

—Michael Sargent

Living life is like running a marathon. It takes a lot of courage and tenacity to keep going till the end.

—Fauja Singh

Running is just you, the work you put in, and the clock. You can't cheat yourself. If you don't put in the miles, you can't go to the starting line thinking you're going to pull a miracle out of nowhere. You get out exactly as much as you put in.

—Desiree Davila Linden

MARATHONS

THE MOST CHALLENGING FEAT A
runner can pursue is the marathon. The 26.2-mile
race has its origin in an ancient Greek legend in
which the messenger Pheidippides ran this length to
Athen to report news of a victory over the Persians
before collapsing and dying from exhaustion. The
race pushes the body—and mind—to its limits.

The difference between the mile and the marathon is the difference between burning your fingers with a match and being slowly roasted over hot coals.

—HAL HIGDON

If you feel bad at 10 miles, you're in trouble. If you feel bad at 20 miles, you're normal. If you don't feel bad at 26 miles, you're abnormal.

—ROBERT DE CASTELLA

You have to forget your last marathon before you try another. Your mind can't know what's coming.

—FRANK SHORTER

The marathon is a charismatic event. It has everything. It has drama. It has competition. Every jogger can't dream of being an Olympic champion, but he can dream of finishing a marathon.

—FRED LEBOW

You don't run 26 miles at five minutes a mile on good looks and a secret recipe.

—FRANK SHORTER

Anyone can run 20 miles. It's the next six that count.

—BARRY MAGEE

Know why people run marathons? (...) Because running is rooted in our collective imagination, and our imagination is rooted in running. Language, art, science; space shuttles, Starry Night, intravascular surgery; they all had their roots in our ability to run. Running was the superpower that made us human—which means it's a superpower all humans possess.

—CHRISTOPHER MCDOUGALL

Training for a marathon is much like climbing a ladder. Each ring is a short-term goal that must be met in sequence in order to reach the long-term goal at the top of the ladder.

—RICHARD BENYO

When you run the marathon, you run against the distance, not against the other runners, and not against the time.

—HAILE GEBRSELASSIE

A runner's creed: I will win; if I cannot win, I shall be second; if I cannot be second, I shall be third; if I cannot place at all, I shall still do my best.

—KEN DOHERTY

The marathon is an art; the marathoner is an artist.

—KIYOSHI NAKAMURA

To describe the agony of a marathon to someone who's never run it is like trying to explain color to someone who was born blind.

—JEROME DRAYTON

You can run a sprint or you can run a marathon, but you can't sprint a marathon.

—RYAN HOLMES

If you want to run, then run a mile. If you want to experience another life, run a marathon.

—EMIL ZATOPEK

The marathon is a competition between your will and your possibilities.

—JEFF GALLOWAY

There is something about the ritual of the race—putting on the number, lining up, being timed —that brings out the best in us.

—GRETE WAITZ

Everyone wins the marathon. We all have the same feeling at the start—nervous, anxious, excited. It is a broader, richer, and even with twenty-seven thousand people—more intimate experience than I found when racing in track.

—GRETE WAITZ

The marathon's about being in contention over the last 10K. That's when it's about what you have in your core. You have run all the strength, all the superficial fitness out of yourself, and it really comes down to what's left inside you. To be able to draw deep and pull something out of yourself is one of the most tremendous things about the marathon.

—ROBERT DE CASTELLA

It can be said that the first half of the marathon is 20 miles long; the second half, 6.2 more.

—HAL HIGDON

No doubt a brain and some shoes are essential for marathon success, although if it comes down to a choice, pick the shoes. More people finish marathons with no brains than with no shoes.

—DON KARDONG

There is the truth about the marathon and very few of you have written the truth. Even if I explain to you, you'll never understand it, you're outside of it.

—DOUGLAS WAKIIHURI

Of all the races, there is no better stage for heroism than a marathon.

—George Sheehan

A marathon is a like a roller coaster…You might toss your cookies, jump for joy, pass out, or have to close your eyes and just breathe. Even when it is going smooth, all of a sudden there can be a drop or even better, an acceleration. Hang on, stick to your plan, and enjoy every step of the way.

—Carrie Tollefson

The long run is what puts the tiger in the cat.

—Bill Squires

Toeing the starting line of a marathon, regardless of the language you speak, the God you worship, or the color of your skin, we all stand as equals. Perhaps the world would be a better place if more people ran.

—DEAN KARNAZES

If you want to win a race, you have to go a little berserk.

—BILL RODGERS

Only think of two things—the report of the pistol and the tape. When you hear one, run like hell until you break the other.

—SAM MUSSABINI

Like the marathon, life can sometimes be difficult, challenging, and present obstacles; however, if you believe in your dreams and never ever give up, things will turn out for the best.

—MEB KEFLEZIGHI

My goal is to beat yours.

—DATHAN RITZENHEIN

If you are losing faith in human nature, go out and watch a marathon.

—KATHRINE SWITZER

RUNNING AS THERAPY

RUNNING BRINGS CLARITY AND *peace. As you work through the solitary miles, you reach the proverbial runner's high: your body floods with endorphins, making every step seem easy—even exhilarating—and the stress in your life fades away.*

Running has always been a relief and a sanctuary—something that makes me feel good, both physically and mentally. For me it's not so much about the health benefits. Those are great, but I believe that the best thing about running is the joy it brings to life.

—Kara Goucher

Running has taken me in, and continues to comfort, heal, and challenge me in all kinds of magical ways. I am not a "good runner" because I am me. I am a good "me" because I am a runner.

—Kristin Armstrong

Running is the classical road to self-consciousness, self-awareness, and self-reliance.

—NOEL CARROLL

We run, not because we think it is doing us good, but because we enjoy it and cannot help ourselves.

—SIR ROGER BANNISTER

Running long and hard is an ideal antidepressant, since it's hard to run and feel sorry for yourself at the same time. Also, there are those hours of clearheadedness that follow a long run.

—MONTE DAVIS

Running is my private time, my therapy, my religion.

—GAIL W. KISLEVITZ

Running is a gift I give myself almost daily. Even at days when everything seems to go wrong, I treat myself on the satisfaction of a lap of 30 to 40 minutes.

—ARTHUR BLANK

When you put yourself on the line in a race and expose yourself to the unknown, you learn things about yourself that are very exciting.

—DORIS BROWN HERITAGE

So much in life seems inflexible and unchangeable, and part of the joy of running and especially racing is the realization that improvement and progress can be achieved.

—NANCY ANDERSON

Running was like the friend that never left. It was just always there.

—LOLO JONES

What the years have shown me is that running clarifies the thinking process as well as purifies the body. I think best—most broadly and most fully—when I am running.

—AMBY BURFOOT

Running is a thing worth doing not because of the future rewards it bestows, but because of how it feeds our bodies and minds and souls in the present.

—Kevin Nelson

Everyone who has run knows that its most important value is in removing tension and allowing a release from whatever other cares the day may bring.

—Jimmy Carter

Running helps me stay on an even keel and in an optimistic frame of mind.

—Bill Clinton

I run because if I didn't, I'd be sluggish and glum and spend too much time on the couch. I run to breathe the fresh air. I run to explore. I run to escape the ordinary. I run...to savor the trip along the way. Life becomes a little more vibrant, a little more intense. I like that.

—DEAN KARNAZES

The pain of running relieves the pain of living.

—JACQUELINE SIMON GUNN

That's the thing about running: your greatest runs are rarely measured by racing success. They are moments in time when running allows you to see how wonderful your life is.

—KARA GOUCHER

A lot of my ideas come to me more easily when I am running. That is why I like to run in the morning, when there are no distractions... Now some of my best ideas are born on the run.

—GRETE WAITZ

Running in the morning has me appreciate all the choices that come later in the day. The choices I make after running seem healthier, wiser, and kinder.

—DEENA KASTOR

Life can pull you down, but running always lifts you up.

—JENNY HADFIELD

Running has given me the courage to start, the determination to keep trying, and the childlike spirit to have fun along the way. Run often and run long, but never outrun your joy of running.

—JULIE ISPHORDING

There's not a better feeling than when you have found that moment of balance and harmony when both running and life come together. Then you know why you run and that you couldn't live without it.

—JOAN BENOIT

Running is a road to self-awareness and reliance—you can push yourself to extremes and learn the harsh reality of your physical and mental limitations or coast quietly down a solitary path watching the earth spin beneath your feet.

—DORIS BROWN HERITAGE

Me thinks that the moment my legs begin to move, my thoughts begin to flow.

—HENRY DAVID THOREAU

Running sharpens the focus on life and intensifies the emotions. Is there any better reason to do anything?

—ANTON KRUPICKA

If you don't have answers to your problems after a four-hour run, you ain't getting them.

—CHRISTOPHER MCDOUGALL

Running is my meditation, mind flush, cosmic telephone, mood elevator, and spiritual communion.

—LORRAINE MOLLER

Every day is a good day when you run.

—KEVIN NELSON

Running allows me to set my mind free. Nothing seems impossible. Nothing unattainable.

—KARA GOUCHER

I started running around my 30th birthday. I wanted to lose weight; I didn't anticipate the serenity. Being in motion, suddenly my body was busy and so my head could work out some issues I had swept under a carpet of wine and cheese. Good therapy, that's a good run.

—MICHAEL WEATHERLY

Running is one of the best solutions to a clear mind.

—Sasha Azevedo

Defeating those negative instincts that are out to defeat us is the difference between winning and losing—and we all face that battle every day.

—Jesse Owens

FREEDOM &
JOY

RUNNING TAKES YOU ANYWHERE
you decide to go. There are no strictures, no pricey equipment. There is you and there is the road. The freedom of running is joyful and inspiring.

I run because long after my footprints fade away, maybe I will have inspired a few to reject the easy path, hit the trails, put one foot in front of the other, and come to the same conclusion I did: I run because it always takes me where I want to go.

—DEAN KARNAZES

The more restricted our society and work become, the more necessary it will be to find some outlet for this craving for freedom. No one can say, "you must not run faster than this, or jump higher than that." The human spirit is indomitable.

—SIR ROGER BANNISTER

Sometimes I run and I don't even feel the effort of running. I don't even feel the ground. I'm just drifting. Incredible feeling. All the agony and frustration, they're all justified by one moment like that.

—STEVE OVETT

The real purpose in running isn't to win the race, it's to test the limits of the human heart.

—BILL BOWERMAN

It's a treat being a runner, out in the world by yourself with not a soul to make you bad-tempered or tell you what to do.

—ALAN SILLITOE

feel a freedom when I start running.

—Nader al-Masri

run because it's my passion, and not just a sport. Every time I walk out the door, I know why I'm going where I'm going and I'm already focused on that special place where I find my peace and solitude. Running, to me, is more than just a physical exercise… it's a consistent reward for victory!

—Sasha Azevedo

For me, running is about freedom. I find that the freer I feel, the faster I am.

—Jennifer Beals

When you run in places you visit, you encounter things you'd never see otherwise.

—TOM BROKAW

I run to feel complete, to feel alive, to feel happy, and to feel free. I run to visit beautiful places, to overcome my fears, and to remind myself—and others—that our limits may not be where we think they are.

—CHRISSIE WELLINGTON

Go fast enough to get there, but slow enough to see.

—JIMMY BUFFETT

Do the work. Do the analysis. But feel your run. Feel your race. Feel the joy that is running.

—KARA GOUCHER

The beauty of running is its simplicity; the beauty of runners is that we all have a similar drive to improve.

—DEENA KASTOR

I believe in the runner's high, and I believe that those who are passionate about running are the ones who experience it to the fullest degree possible. To me, the runner's high is a sensational reaction to a great run! It's an exhilarating feeling of satisfaction and achievement.

—SASHA AZEVEDO

I don't think about the miles that are coming down the road, I don't think about the mile I'm on right now, I don't think about the miles I've already covered. I think about what I'm doing right now, just being lost in the moment.

—RYAN HALL

The freedom of cross country is so primitive. It's woman vs. nature.

—LYNN JENNINGS

In the midst of regular life, running is the touchstone that breathes adventure into my soul.

—KRISTIN ARMSTRONG

Running gives freedom. When you run you can determine your own tempo. You can choose your own course and think whatever you want. Nobody tells you what to do.

—Nina Kuscik

You have to wonder at times what you're doing out there. Over the years, I've given myself a thousand reasons to keep running, but it always comes back to where it started. It comes down to self-satisfaction and a sense of achievement.

—Steve Prefontaine

We run when we're scared, we run when we're ecstatic, we run away from our problems and run around for a good time.

—CHRISTOPHER MCDOUGALL

A runner must run with dreams in his heart.
—EMIL ZATOPEK

I always loved running...it was something you could do by yourself, and under your own power. You could go in any direction, fast or slow as you wanted, fighting the wind if you felt like it, seeking out new sights just on the strength of your feet and the courage of your lungs.

—JESSE OWENS

Moving outward is an act of courage, and in my life, running has also been a vehicle of introduction—to people, places, cultures, and animals. I have run races on all seven continents. Running may be the connective tissue, but the true essence of the sport is a passage to a bigger world.

—BART YASSO

I'll be happy if running and I can grow old together.

—HARUKI MURAKAMI

Go in any direction…seeking out new sights just on the strength of your feet and the courage of your lungs.

—PAULA RADCLIFFE

Running! If there's any activity happier, more exhilarating, more nourishing to the imagination, I can't think what it might be.

—Joyce Carol Oates

Jogging is very beneficial. It's good for your legs and your feet. It's also very good for the ground. If makes it feel needed.

—Charles M. Schulz

I loved the feeling of freedom in running, the fresh air, the feeling that the only person I'm competing with is me.

—Wilma Rudolph

Most of us have enough areas in our lives where we have to meet others' expectations. Let your running be about your own hopes and dreams.

—MEB KEFLEZIGHI

The obsession with running is really an obsession with the potential for more and more life.

—GEORGE SHEEHAN

Stadiums are for spectators. We runners have Nature, and that is much better.

—JUHA VAATAINEN

POWERING
THROUGH
OBSTACLES

RUNNERS PUSH THEIR BODIES TO the limits. At the moment it seems impossible to go any further, the runner finds their last store of energy and pushes through to a new level of fitness and endurance.

A lot of people run a race to see who's the fastest. I run to see who has the most guts.

—STEVE PREFONTAINE

Even when you have gone as far as you can, and everything hurts, and you are staring at the specter of self-doubt, you can find a bit more strength deep inside you, if you look closely enough.

—HAL HIGDON

The body does not want you to do this. As you run, it tells you to stop but the mind must be strong. You always go too far for your body. You must handle the pain with strategy…It is not age; it is not diet. It is the will to succeed.

—JACQUELINE GAREAU

Winning has nothing to do with racing. Most days don't have races anyway. Winning is about struggle and effort and optimism, and never, ever, ever giving up.

—AMBY BURFOOT

What I've learned from running is that the time to push hard is when you're hurting like crazy and you want to give up. Success is often just around the corner.

—JAMES DYSON

Struggling and suffering are the essence of a life worth living. If you're not pushing yourself beyond the comfort zone, if you're not demanding more from yourself—expanding and learning as you go—you're choosing a numb existence. You're denying yourself an extraordinary trip.

—DEAN KARNAZES

Running hills breaks up your rhythm and forces your muscles to adapt to new stresses. The result? You become stronger.

—EAMONN COGHLAN

Persistence is the soul of a champion.

—ALAN WEBB

Your body will argue that there is no justifiable reason to continue. Your only recourse is to call on your spirit, which fortunately functions independently of logic.

—TIM NOAKES

All runners are tough. Everyone has to have a little fire in them that, even in tough times, can't be turned off.

—SHALANE FLANAGAN

Perhaps I don't give the impression that I'm hurting on the track. But that is because I am animated by an interior force which covers my suffering.

—NOUREDDINE MORCELI

When you first get a hill in sight, look at the top of it only once. Then imagine yourself at the bottom of the other side.

—FLORENCE GRIFFITH JOYNER

Ask yourself: "Can I give more?" The answer is usually: "Yes."

—PAUL TERGAT

It's not so much that I began to run, but that I continued.

—HAL HIGDON

I'm inspired by failure. The process of defeat—picking yourself back up again is the hardest thing in the world.

—LOLO JONES

Running is real and relatively simple. But it ain't easy.

—MARK WILL-WEBER

Run like hell and get the agony over with.

—CLARENCE DEMAR

You are truly your own hero in running. It is up to you to have the responsibility and self-discipline to get the job done.

—ADAM GOUCHER

Winning isn't about finishing in first place. It isn't about beating the others. It is about overcoming yourself. Overcoming your body, your limitations, and your fears. Winning means surpassing yourself and turning your dreams into reality.

—KILLIAN JORNET

Running well is a matter of having the patience to persevere when we are tired and not expecting instant results.

—ROBERT DE CASTELLA

Running is a big question mark that's there each and every day. It asks you, "Are you going to be a wimp, or are you going to be strong today?"

—PETER MAHER

As a breed, runners are a pretty gutsy bunch. We constantly push ourselves to discover limitations, then push past them. We want to know how fast we can go, how much pain we can endure, and how far our bodies can carry us before collapsing in exhaustion.

—BART YASSO

Stepping outside the comfort zone is the price I pay to find out how good I can be. If I planned on backing off every time running got difficult I would hang up my shoes and take up knitting.

—DESIREE LINDEN

You can always do more than you think you can.

—JOHN WOODEN

It does not matter how slowly you go as long as you do not stop.

—CONFUCIUS

Running isn't a sport for pretty boys…It's about the sweat in your hair and the blisters on your feet. It's the frozen spit on your chin and the nausea in your gut. It's about throbbing calves and cramps at midnight that are strong enough to wake the dead. It's about getting out the door and running when the rest of the world is only dreaming about having the passion that you need to live each and every day with. It's about being on a lonely road and running like a champion even when there's not a single soul in sight to cheer you on. Running is all about having the desire to train and persevere until every fiber in your legs, mind, and heart is turned to steel. And when you've finally forged hard enough, you will have become the best runner you can be. And that's all that you can ask for.

—Paul Maurer

When it's pouring rain and you're bowling along through the wet, there's satisfaction in knowing you're out there and the others aren't.

—PETER SNELL

Part of a runner's training consists of pushing back the limits of his mind.

—KENNY MOORE

Being defeated is often a temporary condition. Giving up is what makes it permanent.

—MARILYN VOS SAVANT

Cross Country: No half times, no time outs, no substitutions. It must be the only true sport.

—CHUCK NORRIS

Hills are speed-work in disguise.

—FRANK SHORTER

We all have bad days and bad workouts, when running gets ugly, when split times seem slow, when you wonder why you started. It will pass.

—HAL HIGDON

In football, you might get your bell rung, but you go in with the expectation that you might get hurt, and you hope to win and come out unscathed. As a distance runner, you know you're going to get your bell rung. Distance runners are experts at pain, discomfort, and fear. You're not coming away feeling good. It's a matter of how much pain you can deal with on those days. It's not a strategy. It's just a callusing of the mind and body to deal with discomfort. Any serious runner bounces back. That's the nature of their game. Taking pain.

—MARK WETMORE

Challenges are meant to be met and overcome.
—LIU XIANG

Conclusion

RUNNING IS A LIFELONG endeavor. The sport doesn't just belong to elite athletes. Everyone who laces up their shoes and takes a lap around their neighborhood is a runner. Having the will to keep at it, mile after mile, day after day, year after year, is what makes the sport so rewarding. In this way, running is a microcosm of your life: it's not the destination that's important, it's the entire arc of the journey.

Your motivation for continuing the sport changes and evolves over time, as do your individual goals. What began as a desire for better overall health may awaken a spirit of competition, whether among others or within yourself. In running a race or even completing a marathon, you realize your incredible potential. The sport reveals an astonishing truth to you: you are the master of your route; there's a freedom and joy in this discovery.

Injury may slow your gait; life may disrupt your running routine or pause it for a period of time. No matter. The next run is always there waiting for you.

<u>Also Available</u>

The Joy of Cycling
The Joy of Swimming